This notebook belongs to:

Published by Sirimiri Publishing

Made in the USA
Middletown, DE
10 September 2022

10197550R10068